Danny D was naughty.
That made Daddy sad.
Danny and Daddy talked about it.
Daddy said, "Danny D,
God is **never** naughty and he
wants his children to be like him."

"Never, never, **never** naughty?"
asked Danny D.
"Never, never, **never** naughty."
said Daddy.

Danny D was so sorry he had
been naughty. He asked Daddy
and God to forgive him.

That helped.
Danny D
felt happy again.

BUT . . .

The next day Danny D and Christy were fighting. Danny D took Christy's book just when she wanted to read it. Danny D didn't really want the book. He just didn't want Christy to have it either.

Mommy heard all the fuss. She very quietly said, "Danny D, God never took things that didn't belong to him." Then she left the room.

Danny D was
sorry he had
teased Christy.
He gave her
the book
and a big hug.

Christy smiled
and Danny D
was happy too.

BUT . . .

The next day Danny D
opened a box
his Mommy had told
him not to touch.
He played with some
of the treasures inside
and made a mess.
"Danny D, have you been
playing with my things
in that box I told you
not to touch?"
Mommy asked.
"No!" said Danny D.

That was a lie,
wasn't it?

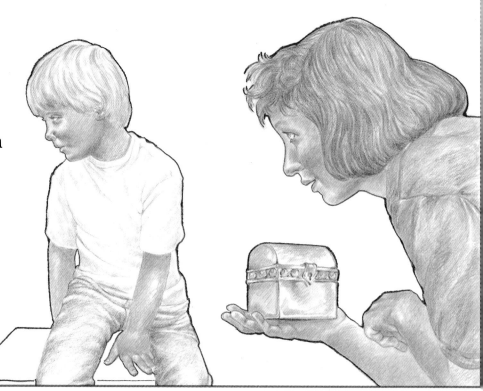

Danny D felt **AWFUL** because he knew he
had done two wrong things.
First, he played with Mommy's treasures.
Second, he lied to Mommy.
Danny D remembered that
God never tells lies.
And God wants us
to be like him.

So-o-o-o
Danny D asked God to forgive him.
Then Danny D told Mommy he was sorry
for the two naughty things he had done.

Mommy and Danny D
sat on the steps and
talked and talked
about good things and bad things
and how God is
never, never, **never**
naughty and he wants us
to be like him.

Mommy gave Danny D a big kiss
and said, "I love you, Danny D."

BUT . . . The next day Danny D's Cousin Drew was visiting and Cousin Drew wanted to watch Sesame Street on TV. Danny D wanted to watch cartoons.

They argued and argued. Danny D got very, very, **very** angry! He shouted! Drew yelled! Both of them had a red face and a mean look.

Papa Stu heard the commotion. Both Danny D and Cousin Drew wanted their own way. Selfish, angry, unkind—both of them!

Papa Stu patted both their heads.
He put an arm around each one.
Then he stooped down so he could
see right into Danny D's
and Cousin Drew's eyes.
Papa Stu very quietly said,
"Both of you know that God
wouldn't get mad, and shout
if he couldn't watch
what he wanted."

Two heads
hung down.